BRIGHT IDEA BOOKS

COLIN
Kaepernick

by Stephanie Watson

CAPSTONE PRESS
a capstone imprint

Bright Idea Books are published by Capstone Press
1710 Roe Crest Drive, North Mankato, Minnesota 56003
www.mycapstone.com

Library of Congress Cataloging-in-Publication Data
Names: Watson, Stephanie, 1969- author.
Title: Colin Kaepernick / by Stephanie Watson.
Description: North Mankato, Minnesota : Bright Idea Books are published by
  Capstone Press, [2019] | Series: Influential People | Includes
  bibliographical references and index.
Identifiers: LCCN 2018019492 (print) | LCCN 2018024429 (ebook) | ISBN
  9781543541687 (ebook) | ISBN 9781543541281 (hardcover : alk. paper)
Subjects: LCSH: Kaepernick, Colin, 1987---Juvenile literature. | Quarterbacks
  (Football)--United States--Biography--Juvenile literature. | Black lives
  matter movement--Juvenile literature. | Football--Social aspects.
Classification: LCC GV939.K25 (ebook) | LCC GV939.K25 W37 2019 (print) | DDC
  796.332092 [B] --dc23
LC record available at https://lccn.loc.gov/2018019492

Editorial Credits
Editor: Mirella Miller
Designer: Becky Daum
Production Specialist: Megan Ellis

J-B
KAEPERNICK
460-3885

Quote Sources
p. 20, "Jaworski: Kaepernick 'Could Be One of Greatest Quarterbacks Ever.'" *CBS Sports*, August 22, 2013; p. 22, "Colin Kaepernick: 'We Are Under Attack.'" *247Sports*, July 7, 2016

Photo Credits
AP Images: Marcio Jose Sanchez, cover; Getty Images: Al Diaz/Miami Herald/Tribune News Service, 5; Icon Sportswire: Allan Hamilton, 14–15, Brian Rothmuller, 24, Marc Sanchez, 17, Mark Goldman, 8–9, Tony Medina, 18–19, 20–21; Newscom: Erik McGregor/Sipa USA, 26–27; Shutterstock Images: Jeff Bukowski, 6–7, Jstone, 23, 28, Stephen Coburn, 31; Yearbook Library: Seth Poppel, 11, 12–13

Design Elements: iStockphoto, Red Line Editorial, and Shutterstock Images

TABLE OF CONTENTS

CHAPTER ONE
TAKE A KNEE 4

CHAPTER TWO
THREE-SPORT ATHLETE..... 10

CHAPTER THREE
ROAD TO THE NFL 16

CHAPTER FOUR
KAEPERNICK PROTESTS..... 22

Glossary 28
Timeline................................ 29
Activity 30
Further Resources............... 32
Index..................................... 32

CHAPTER 1

TAKE A
Knee

It was September 1, 2016. The football game was about to start. The San Francisco 49ers were playing. The San Diego Chargers faced off against them. Everyone stood for the national anthem. But one 49ers player did not stand. Colin Kaepernick kneeled.

Kaepernick (right) kneels during the national anthem on November 27, 2016.

Football fans followed
Kaepernick's example
and kneeled.

Kaepernick kneeled in **protest**. He did not like the way police treated black people. He believed the police shot people because of their skin color. He wanted everyone to know these actions were wrong.

ATHLETES PROTESTING

Kaepernick is not the only athlete to protest. Boxer Muhammad Ali spoke out against war.

Kaepernick was not alone. Some of his teammates joined him. In the next few weeks, other football players kneeled too. Some players locked arms in protest. Others raised their fists to the sky. Soccer and basketball players also kneeled.

Other football players also began kneeling in support of Kaepernick.

NO RESPECT

Not everyone agreed with Kaepernick. Some said he did not respect the United States. Others thought he did not respect the flag. People thought his kneeling upset soldiers who fought wars. Some people booed Kaepernick at football games. He still did not stop. He did what he thought was right.

CHAPTER 2

THREE-SPORT Athlete

Kaepernick was born in 1987.

His parents adopted him. Kaepernick

has one brother and one sister.

Kaepernick played football, basketball, and baseball. He threw footballs farther than other kids. He pitched baseballs as fast as a pro. He scored more than 30 points a game in basketball.

Kaepernick had a happy and active childhood.

Football has always
been Kaepernick's
favorite sport.

Kaepernick was a star athlete in high school. He was great in his three sports. But he liked football best. He played **quarterback.**

CALL ME BO

Kaepernick's brother called him Bo growing up. The name came from Bo Jackson. Jackson was a famous athlete. He also played football and baseball.

Kaepernick's fourth-grade dream would one day come true!

Kaepernick wrote a letter to himself in fourth grade. He made a guess. One day he would play in the National Football League (NFL). He would be a famous quarterback.

CHAPTER 3

ROAD TO
the NFL

Three colleges wanted Kaepernick to play baseball. But he wanted to play football.

Kaepernick played with the University of Nevada Wolf Pack.

Kaepernick gained many fans during his college football career.

The University of Nevada wanted Kaepernick to play football. He joined the team in 2007. Kaepernick sat on the bench at first. The Wolf Pack already had a quarterback. His name was Nick Graziano.

One day Graziano broke his foot during a game. Kaepernick took over. Nevada lost the game. But Kaepernick scored five touchdowns.

Kaepernick played for four seasons. He broke college football records. He passed for more than 10,000 yards. He ran for more than 4,000 yards. He was the only college player to do both.

DRAFT PICK

The 49ers **drafted** Kaepernick in 2011. He led them to the Super Bowl in his second season.

Kaepernick calls a play during the 2013 Super Bowl.

One sports reporter thought Kaepernick had a big future. He said Kaepernick could be "one of the greatest quarterbacks ever."

CHAPTER 4

KAEPERNICK
Protests

Kaepernick started reading about **civil rights**. He thought police treated black people unfairly. He was angry. He wrote on Instagram, "We are under attack!"

Kaepernick thought it was important to be educated on the problems in the United States.

Kaepernick began to sit during the national anthem. No one noticed. Then he kneeled. Other players kneeled too. People noticed. Some fans got mad. They sent angry letters to Kaepernick. Some letters were **racist**.

Some fans did not agree with Kaepernick protesting.

A HARD SEASON

It was not a good season for the 49ers. They won only two games in 2016. Kaepernick played well. He threw 16 touchdown passes.

Kaepernick kept protesting. He donated $1 million to help people of color. His team gave him an award for having courage.

#IMWITHKAP

Some New York police officers held a **rally**. It honored Kaepernick. They wore black shirts. The shirts said #IMWITHKAP.

Many people respected Kaepernick's actions.

WHITE SILENCE = WHITE VIOLENCE

TAKE A KNEE AGAINST POLICE BRUTALITY

RISEANDRESIST.ORG

FREE AGENT

Kaepernick left the 49ers in March 2017. He could play for any team that wanted him. But no team hired him. Team owners said he spent too much time protesting. They said his **focus** needed to be on football.

Kaepernick still did not have a team in 2018. Yet people knew his name. He had knelt to take a stand.

GLOSSARY

civil rights
a person's right to be free
and equal to others

drafted
invited to play on a
sports team

focus
paying attention

protest
standing up against
something you believe
is wrong

quarterback
the football player who calls
the plays and throws the ball

racist
treating people differently
because of their skin color

rally
come together to
support someone

TIMELINE

1987: Colin Kaepernick is born in Milwaukee, Wisconsin.

2002: Kaepernick starts high school in Turlock, California.

2006: Kaepernick attends the University of Nevada, Reno.

2011: The San Francisco 49ers draft Kaepernick.

2016: Kaepernick kneels during the national anthem in protest.

2017: Kaepernick becomes a free agent.

ACTIVITY

CONDUCT AN INTERVIEW

Interview your school physical education teacher or coach. Write the interview as a news story. Or record it on video.

ASK QUESTIONS SIMILAR TO THESE:

What makes a great athlete?

How does someone become a great athlete?

What are the best ways to become better at sports?

FURTHER RESOURCES

Love learning about Colin Kaepernick? Learn more here:

Colin Kaepernick. NFL.com
http://www.nfl.com/player/colinkaepernick/2495186/profile

Doeden, Matt. *Football's Greatest Quarterbacks*. North Mankato, Minn.: Capstone, 2015.

Fishman, Jon M. *Colin Kaepernick*. Minneapolis: Lerner Publications, 2015.

Hoblin, Paul. *Colin Kaepernick*. Minneapolis: ABDO Publishing, 2014.

Inspired by Kaepernick's protest? Find out more about it here:

Teaching Kids News: What's the "Take a Knee" Controversy All About?
http://teachingkidsnews.com/2017/10/01/whats-take-knee-controversy/

INDEX

Ali, Muhammad, 7

civil rights, 22

Graziano, Nick, 18–19

Jackson, Bo, 13

Kaepernick, Colin
college records, 19
family, 10
high school sports, 11, 13
national anthem, 4, 24
National Football League (NFL), 15

police, 7, 22, 25

San Diego Chargers, 4

San Francisco 49ers, 4, 20, 25, 27

Super Bowl, 20

University of Nevada, 18–19